Thank you!!

I know that you are eager to read my book, but I just wanted to say thank you for purchasing it.

Slimming down from 19 stones to 12 stones was not easy, especially due to my passionate love of food! Developing the recipes in this book genuinely changed my life as they allowed me to tackle my weight without sacrificing my favorite tastes.

I am deeply honored to share these recipes with you and I hope they will help you to lose weight as well.

If you have the time, please leave a review on Amazon. I don't have the time or money to compete with established publishers. Posting a review would help greatly in spreading the word!!

Post a review here:
http://bit.ly/lowcarbreview
(You will be asked to sign in to your Amazon account.)

Also, if you ever want to get in touch, please email me (address at end of book). I will be happy to give you whatever help I can in your weight loss goals.

Love

Sabrina Hartford.

Free Gift + Free Future Books: Expires soon!

Congratulations! If you can read this message, then your purchase qualifies for the free *Suggested Accompaniments* chart.

Have you ever wanted to add something to your dessert? Maybe:
- A few blueberries on the side?
- A scoop of ice cream?
- A sprinkling of nuts?
- A spray of cream?

Be careful! These additions could massively inflate your carb and calorie intake!

Our chart illustrates the carb and calorie values of the most popular dessert accompaniments. It is elegantly designed, so you can print it out and pin it up in your kitchen for easy access to this vital information. That way, you'll know exactly which additions are safe to have!

This free gift will be deleted from future editions of the book and sold as a separate item with an RRP of $9.99. When this happens, it will no longer be free for you, so please take action now to secure your copy.

To receive your gift, simply validate your email address at
http://bit.ly/lowcarbclub

In order to receive your gift, you will need to sign up for our free email newsletter, which details our new books. Don't worry about spam: We only send the newsletter occasionally, usually once a year.

Don't undo all your hard work with an innocent mistake. Download today!

Contents

Free Gift + Free Future Books:
Expires soon!..2
Don't let sweeteners wreck your diet!......................5
Tips & Tricks..7
1) Buttermilk Chocolate Fudge..................................8
2) Crêpes..10
3) Almond Ice Cream..12
4) Sunflower Waffles..14
5) Almond Banana Bread..16
6) Mixed Berry Fool..18
7) Giant Crunchy Pumpkin Cookies........................20
8) Peanut Butter Protein Cookies............................22
9) Chocoholic Cookies...24
10) No Cook Chocolate Peanut Butter Protein Balls..26
11) No Cook Cocoa Bars...28
12) Almond Pie Crust...30
13) Cheesecake..32
14) Cinnamon Berry Pie..34
15) Creamy Lemon Pie..36
16) Pumpkin Pie..38
17) Crumbling Nutmeg Muffins.................................40
18) Cinnamon Muffins..42
19) Mixed Berry Layer Cake.....................................44
20) Berry Chocolate Cake...46
21) Apricot Cocoa Cake...50

22) Carrot Cake 52

Easily rewire your mindset:
Use desserts as tools to both succeed at your diet and change your whole life 54

Mindset tool 1:
Make desserts a reward for forming new habits 55

Mindset tool 2:
Dessert scheduling 58

Mindset tool 3:
Savor preparation 59

Mindset tool 4:
Make dessert eating a ritual 60

Mindset tool 5:
Form the habit of gratitude 62

Free Gift + Free Future Books:
Expires soon! 64

Join my Facebook recipe group! 65

Check out my other dessert books 66

Check out my dessert mystery books 68

Enjoy this book: Yes/No?
– Contact the author 71

Freebies & Offers 73

About the author 74

Don't forget to leave a review! 75

Copyright 76

Don't let sweeteners wreck your diet!

Most low carb diets encourage the use of artificial sweeteners. This seems logical, as natural sugars are both high in carbs and calories.

Unfortunately, artificial sweeteners have 3 key problems.

1) Artificial sweeteners get stored by the body

Artificial sweeteners are not natural, so your body does not know how to process them. Instead of breaking them down, it simply stores them resulting in weight gain.

2) Artificial sweeteners lower fat burning abilities

Susan Swithers, a professor of behavioral neuroscience at Purdue University, has conducted many studies into sweeteners.

According to her, sweet foods contain extra calories in comparison to other foods. When the tongue receives a sweet taste, the brain sends signals to the gut to enter a 'preparation state' so it can digest the extra calories.

Sweeteners do not have any calories, so the body gets confused. It prepares itself to burn the extra calories, but nothing happens. Over time, the body retrains itself not to enter this preparation state, which lowers its effectiveness at fat burning.

3) Sweeteners encourage overeating

The act of burning calories triggers a feeling of satisfaction, which encourages a person to stop eating.

Sweeteners skip this process making it harder to feel full.

Not convinced? – Check out these studies!

A number of studies have shown the harmful effects of sweeteners:

Swithers & Davidson in *The Journal of Behavioral Neuroscience* (2008):
This study showed that artificial sweeteners trigger physiological and hormonal responses in the body that increase weight.

Appetite Journal (2013):
This study demonstrated increased weight gain from using sweeteners.

Nature Journal (2014):
In this study, people who used sweeteners had increased blood sugar, which in some cases, were at pre-diabetic levels.

Yale Journal of Biology and Medicine (2010):
A link between obesity and sweeteners was demonstrated in this study.

Don't ruin your diet!

All the recipes in this book use ZERO sweeteners, so you don't have to worry about wrecking your diet. Our ingredients contain just enough calories to allow your body to process them healthily without making you overweight.

Of course, you still need to eat in moderation, so we've also listed carb counts and nutritional information for each recipe. You can enjoy your favorite treats as often as you like, provided you keep an eye on these values to pace yourself.

As we use no sweeteners, you will need to take care to refrigerate the desserts.

Tips & Tricks

Vanilla

All recipes in this book make reference to vanilla bean pods.

Use the tip of a sharp knife to cut the pod down the seam and then use the same knife to scrape the seeds out. These can then be sprinkled into your dessert for maximum flavor.

Another option is to grind the extracted seeds into a fine powder using a mortar and pestle. You can then mix them into a liquid (such as milk or water) before including them in the dessert.

If you don't have any pods, you can also substitute 1 bean pod with 1 tsp of vanilla extract (although refer to the bottle, as the strength of the extract can vary).

Don't throw away the empty pods: Place them in a sugar jar to add delicious vanilla flavors to your sugar!

Regional Differences

All ingredients in this book are listed by their American names.

Here are the regional equivalents for international readers:
Confectioners' sugar = Icing/powdered sugar
Granulated sugar = Caster sugar
All-purpose flour = Plain flour
Heavy whipping cream = Double cream
Lamington tin = Shallow long cake tin

All measurements are provided in imperial and metric. Unless otherwise stated, measurements list total amounts (So *'2 large (30ml) egg yolks'* means the total of the two yolks is 30ml). You can substitute regular sized eggs and fruits with large versions (and vice-versa) without any major differences to the taste.

1) Buttermilk Chocolate Fudge

Chocolate fudge with an unique creamy buttery taste.

Net carbs: 2.5g per large serving
Makes 12 large servings

Ingredients

½ cup (120ml) buttermilk
¼ cup (55g) coconut oil
¼ cup (60ml) heavy cream (double cream)
1 cup (230g) organic chocolate pieces (70% cocoa)*
*You can use other chocolates, but select ones with a high cocoa value, as these have less sugar and so lower carb counts.

Steps

1. Pour the buttermilk, coconut oil and heavy cream into a saucepan.
2. Cook on a low heat, occasionally stirring. Cook until all the ingredients are combined.
3. Add the chocolate pieces. Stir regularly to allow the chocolate to fully melt.
4. Pour the mixture into a tray lined with baking paper.
5. When cool, place in a refrigerator for 1 to 2 hours.

Shopping list

Purchase specialty ingredients on Amazon:

Buttermilk (liquid):	https://amzn.to/2zjTzmp
Coconut oil:	https://amzn.to/2NwYOCl
Organic chocolate pieces:	https://amzn.to/2N0AyaA

Nutritional information (per serving)

Calories 93   (From Fat 76)
Total Fat 8.4g   (daily 13%)
Saturated Fat 6.0g   (daily 30%)
Cholesterol 3mg   (daily 1%)
Sodium 2mg   (daily 0%)
Potassium 1mg   (daily 0%)
Carbohydrates 3.4g   (daily 1%)
Dietary Fiber 0.9g   (daily 4%)
Sugars 2.8g
Protein 1.2g

2) Crêpes

A delicious easy-to-make variation of the classic recipe.

Net carbs: 2.8g per crêpe
Makes 11 crêpes

Ingredients

1.5 oz (45g) ricotta cheese
1.5 oz (45g) yoghurt
5 large (285g) eggs
2 tbsp (30ml) coconut flour
1 tbsp (15ml) oat flour
½ vanilla bean

Steps

1. Using a food processor, blend the ricotta cheese and yoghurt to slightly loosen them up.
2. Add the eggs to the mixture and briefly blend again.
3. Add the coconut flour, oat flour and vanilla.
4. Blend for approximately 1 minute until a smooth mixture is formed.
5. Place approximately 3 tablespoons of the mixture into a non-stick pan, which will form a single crêpe. You may need to add extra spoons to properly form the crêpe.
6. Rotate the pan around so the mixture covers it fully. Use the back of a spatula to pat it down.
7. Cook on a medium heat.
8. Flip the crêpe over (using a spatula) and cook the other side. It only needs a couple of seconds.

Shopping list

Purchase specialty ingredients on Amazon:

Ricotta cheese:	**https://amzn.to/2zooOwH**
Coconut flour:	**https://amzn.to/2KZ9QSj**
Oat flour:	**https://amzn.to/2uh44B6**
Vanilla bean:	**https://amzn.to/2KSuOCd**

Nutritional information (per serving)

Calories 174	(from Fat 127)
Total Fat 14.1g	(daily 22%)
Saturated Fat 2.7g	(daily 14%)
Cholesterol 152mg	(daily 51%)
Sodium 316mg	(daily 13%)
Potassium 98mg	(daily 3%)
Carbohydrates 4.2g	(daily 1%)
Dietary Fiber 1.4g	(daily 6%)
Sugars 1.4g	
Protein 9.3g	

3) Almond Ice Cream

Delicious ice cream with a nutty twist.

Net carbs: 5.7g per scoop
Makes 30 scoops

Ingredients

5 large (285g) eggs
½ cup (175g) honey
1 vanilla bean
2 cups (500ml) heavy cream (double cream)
1 cup (170g) almonds

Steps

1. Crack the eggs and separate the yolks from the whites.
2. Use a whisk to beat the egg yolks into a creamy mixture.
3. While beating the eggs, gradually add half of the honey.
4. Add the vanilla.
5. In a separate bowl, whisk the cream. An electric whisk works best. (You can do it by hand but it will take longer). As the cream starts to thicken, increase the speed.
6. It will start to become foamy and soft peaks will eventually form. When ready, the peaks should bend when you stop whisking. Be sure to check at regular intervals, as if you whisk too long, you will be left with a butter-like substance!
7. In a separate dry bowl, beat the egg whites until soft peaks form.
8. Once the peaks form, slowly pour in the remaining honey while beating.
9. Continue beating until the mixture is thick.
10. Take 3 tablespoons of the cream mixture and fold it into the egg whites and gently stir. Repeat this until the mixture is used up.
11. Skin and chop the almonds.
12. Add the almonds and gently stir to ensure all has mixed.
13. Spoon into a container.
14. Freeze overnight until firm. Cover the container for best results.

Variations

You can replace the almonds with virtually any type of nut with only a minor increase in carbs.

Shopping list

Purchase specialty ingredients on Amazon:

Almonds: https://amzn.to/2KIcsVk

Vanilla bean: https://amzn.to/2KSuOCd

Nutritional information (per serving)

Calories 106   (from Fat 77)
Total Fat 8.6g   (daily 13%)
Saturated Fat 4.3g   (daily 21%)
Cholesterol 58mg   (daily 19%)
Sodium 14mg   (daily 01%)
Potassium 51mg   (daily 01%)
Carbohydrates 6.1g   (daily 02%)
Dietary Fiber 0.4g   (daily 02%)
Sugars 5.0g
Protein 2.1g

4) Sunflower Waffles

The unusual ingredient of sunflower seeds creates a delicious and unique twist to a well-loved recipe.

Net carbs: 3.7g per waffle
Makes 5 waffles

Ingredients

3 tbsp (12g) sunflower seeds
½ cup (50g) almond flour
4 large (228g) eggs
½ cup (125g) low-fat ricotta
1 tsp (6ml) lemon juice
¼ tsp (1.5g) sea salt
½ tsp (2.4g) baking soda
1 tbsp (15ml) olive oil

Steps

1. Using a food processor, blend the sunflower seeds into flour.
2. Add all the ingredients (except for the olive oil) and blend for approximately 1 minute. The mixture should be bubbly.
3. Add the olive oil and blend for another 30 seconds.
4. The mixture is now ready to use in your waffle maker. The instructions vary between each model, but usually you just pour it and turn it on.

Variations

You can swap the sunflower seeds with almond flour. Try also swapping the olive oil with warmed coconut oil for a unique flavor. None of these changes will significantly effect the carbs.

Shopping list

Purchase specialty ingredients on Amazon:

Sunflower seeds:	https://amzn.to/2znjD05
Almond flour:	https://amzn.to/2MXcd5t
Low-fat ricotta (not always available):	https://amzn.to/2L394k5

Nutritional information (per serving)

Calories 201 (from Fat 135)
Total Fat 15.1g (daily 23%)
Saturated Fat 3.9g (daily 29%)
Cholesterol 156mg (daily 52%)
Sodium 338mg (daily 14%)
Potassium 86mg (daily 2%)
Carbohydrates 6.7g (daily 2%)
Dietary Fiber 3.0g (daily 12%)
Sugars 1.1g
Protein 11.2g

5) Almond Banana Bread

Mmmmm..... Making this bread fills your home with a mouth-watering smell!

Net carbs: 7.5g per slice
Makes 16 slices

Ingredients

½ cup (70g) almond flour
1 tsp (4.8g) baking soda
½ cup (70g) coconut flour
½ tsp (3g) sea salt
1 medium (120g) banana
½ cup (110g) coconut oil
4 large (228g) eggs
¼ cup (85g) honey
½ vanilla bean
½ cup (60g) almonds

Steps

1. Preheat the oven to 350°F (180°C).
2. Mix the almond flour, baking soda, coconut flour and sea salt.
3. Using a food processor, blend the banana to form a purée.
4. In a separate bowl, mix the banana purée, coconut oil, eggs, honey and vanilla to form a smooth batter. Pour this bowl into the first.
5. Skin the almonds and chop them into small pieces.
6. Add the chopped almonds to the bowl. Mix until all ingredients have completely combined.
7. Grease a loaf tin with butter and pour the batter into it.
8. Bake for approximately 40 minutes. When ready, you can put a knife in the centre and it will come out clean.

Shopping list

Purchase specialty ingredients on Amazon:

Almond flour:	https://amzn.to/2J7kPUP
Coconut oil:	https://amzn.to/2MXjxht
Almonds:	https://amzn.to/2KYfNf3

Nutritional information (per serving)

Calories 148 (from Fat 101)
Total Fat 11.2g (daily 17%)
Saturated Fat 7.6g (daily 38%)
Cholesterol 41mg (daily 14%)
Sodium 171mg (daily 07%)
Potassium 69mg (daily 02%)
Carbohydrates 10.0g (daily 03%)
Dietary Fiber 2.5g (daily 10%)
Sugars 5.7g
Protein 3.4g

6) Mixed Berry Fool

A delicious creamy, berry explosion.

Net carbs: 5.6g per serving
Makes 5 servings

Ingredients

1 cup (230g) heavy cream (double cream)
3 cups (375g) mixed berries (strawberries, raspberries, blueberries)
1 tbsp (18ml) rosewater

Steps

1. Place the heavy cream in a large bowl.
2. Using a whisk, slowly beat the cream. An electric whisk works best (You can do it by hand but it will take longer).
3. As the cream starts to thicken, increase the speed.
4. It will become foamy and a peak will eventually form. When ready, the peak should bend when you stop whisking. Be sure to check at regular intervals, as if you whisk too long, you will be left with a butter-like substance!
5. Using a food processor, combine the berries and rosewater. Then blend until the berries are fully liquid.
6. Fill one-third of a tall glass with the liquid berries.
7. Pour in the cream to fill the glass.
8. Add a heaped spoonful of liquid berries on top to finish it off.

Shopping list

Purchase specialty ingredients on Amazon:

Mixed berries: https://amzn.to/2NCXeyB

Rose water: https://amzn.to/2znjg5l

Nutritional information (per serving)

Calories 110 (From Fat 82)
Total Fat 9.1g (daily 14%)
Saturated Fat 5.5g (daily 28%)
Cholesterol 33mg (daily 11%)
Sodium 10mg (daily 0%)
Potassium 150mg (daily 4%)
Carbohydrates 7.3g (daily 2%)
Dietary Fiber 1.7g (daily 07%)
Sugars 4.3g
Protein 1.1g

7) Giant Crunchy Pumpkin Cookies

Crunch! Crunch! These cookies are irresistible, especially as they bake with a rich nutty smell!

Net carbs: 5.8g per cookie
Makes 5 giant cookies

Ingredients

¼ regular sized pumpkin (or ½ cup (300g) of ready-made pumpkin purée)
2 large (114g) eggs
2 tsp (9g) coconut oil
½ vanilla bean
1 tbsp (6g) almond flour
1 tsp (2.6g) nutmeg
1 cup (85g) brazil nuts

Steps

1. Preheat the oven to 350°F (180°C).
2. Using a food processor, blend the pumpkin pieces to form a purée.
   (You can also use ½ cup (300g) of ready made purée but this might have added sugar).
3. In a mixing bowl, whisk the eggs, coconut oil, pumpkin purée and vanilla until completely combined.
4. Add the almond flour and nutmeg.
5. Whisk until thoroughly combined.
6. Chop the brazil nuts into small pieces.
7. Line a tray with baking paper and spread the nuts on it in a single layer.
8. Place the tray in the oven to toast the nuts. You will need to stir the nuts on a regular basis to avoid burning.
9. After approximately 5 minutes, the nuts will be toasted. There should be a delicious nutty smell.
10. Add the toasted nuts to the mixing bowl and briefly whisk again until the mixture completely combines.
11. Line a tray with baking paper.

12. Place a heaped spoonful of the mixture onto the tray to form the giant cookie shape (you may need to add extra spoonfuls to stop the cookies from being too flat).
13. Bake for 15 minutes. The edges should brown.

Shopping list

Purchase specialty ingredients on Amazon:

Pumpkin purée:	https://amzn.to/2u57tUf
Coconut oil:	https://amzn.to/2KIQTE8
Vanilla bean:	https://amzn.to/2KSuOCd
Almond flour:	https://amzn.to/2m3XtX9
Nutmeg:	https://amzn.to/2m7QaxA
Brazil nuts:	https://amzn.to/2JbZiuk

Nutritional information (per serving)

Calories 212	(from Fat 161)
Total Fat 17.9g	(daily 28%)
Saturated Fat 5.0g	(daily 25%)
Cholesterol 66mg	(daily 22%)
Sodium 33mg	(daily 01%)
Potassium 137mg	(daily 04%)
Carbohydrates 9.3g	(daily 03%)
Dietary Fiber 3.5g	(daily 14%)
Sugars 2.9g	
Protein 6.9g	

8) Peanut Butter Protein Cookies

Irresistibly nutty cookies that are bursting with protein.

Net carbs: 2.0g per cookie
Makes 14 cookies

Ingredients

1 tbsp (14g) coconut oil
2 large (114g) eggs
¾ cup (195g) peanut butter
1 cup (125g) vanilla protein powder

Steps

1. Preheat the oven to 350°F (180°C).
2. Whisk the coconut oil, eggs, peanut butter and protein powder to create a thick dough.
3. Roll the dough into small balls.
4. Flatten the balls down slightly to make a cookie shape.
5. Place on a baking tray leaving a 2" (5cm) gap between each cookie.
6. Bake for approximately 5 to 10 minutes until golden brown.

Shopping list

Purchase specialty ingredients on Amazon:

Coconut oil:	https://amzn.to/2u5ou0z
Peanut butter:	https://amzn.to/2uhz6bZ
Vanilla protein powder:	https://amzn.to/2u7ngC9

Nutritional information (per serving)

Calories 99 (from Fat 77)
Total Fat 8.6g (daily 13%)
Saturated Fat 2.5g (daily 13%)
Cholesterol 23mg (daily 8%)
Sodium 72mg (daily 3%)
Potassium 98mg (daily 3%)
Carbohydrates 2.8g (daily 1%)
Dietary Fiber 0.8g (daily 3%)
Sugars 1.4g
Protein 4.2g

9) Chocoholic Cookies

A must for chocolate lovers!

Net carbs: 9.8g per cookie
Makes 30 cookies

Ingredients

1 cup (145g) sunflower seeds
1 tsp (4.8g) baking soda
½ cup (45g) unsweetened cocoa powder
1 tsp (6g) sea salt
1 cup (250g) almond butter
¼ cup (55g) coconut oil
2 large (114g) eggs
¾ cup (255g) honey
1 vanilla bean
1½ cup (250g) organic chocolate pieces (70% cocoa)*
*You can use other chocolates, but select ones with a high cocoa value, as these have less sugar and so lower carb counts.

Steps

1. Preheat the oven to 350°F (180°C).
2. Using a food processor, blend the sunflower seeds into flour.
3. In a separate bowl, mix the blended sunflower seeds, baking soda, coca powder and sea salt.
4. Gently warm the coconut oil so it fully melts. Avoid too much heat to prevent burning.
5. In another separate bowl, mix the almond butter, coconut oil, eggs, honey and vanilla.
6. Combine the two mixtures in a single bowl for a final round of mixing.
7. Line a tray with baking paper.
8. Take 1 tablespoon of the mixture and place it on the tray to form a cookie. You may need to add extra spoons to properly form the cookie shape. Leave approximately a 2" (5cm) gap between the cookies, as they will expand.
9. Bake for around 5 to 10 minutes until the edges become crisp. The cookies should rise slightly before flattening.

10. Place the cookies on a cooling rack until they have hardened.
11. Melt the chocolate pieces.
12. Dip the cookies into the melted chocolate.
13. Refrigerate the cookies to allow them to cool and solidify.

Shopping list

Purchase specialty ingredients on Amazon:

Sunflower seeds:	https://amzn.to/2znjD05
Unsweetened cocoa powder:	https://amzn.to/2uq0sgr
Almond butter:	https://amzn.to/2L1GmQt
Coconut oil:	https://amzn.to/2KUWVAR
Vanilla bean:	https://amzn.to/2ueRMcD
Organic chocolate pieces (70% cocoa) (not always available)	https://amzn.to/2NCGTKr

Nutritional information (per serving)

Calories 143	(from Fat 93)
Total Fat 10.3g	(daily 16%)
Saturated Fat 3.8g	(daily 19%)
Cholesterol 12mg	(daily 4%)
Sodium 110mg	(daily 5%)
Potassium 104mg	(daily 3%)
Carbohydrates 11.3g	(daily 4%)
Dietary Fiber 1.5g	(daily 6%)
Sugars 8.5g	
Protein 3.3g	

10) No Cook Chocolate Peanut Butter Protein Balls

Not only are these lovely balls absolutely scrumptious, they also don't require any cooking!

Net carbs: 1.5g per ball
Makes 18 balls

Ingredients

¼ cup (20g) unsweetened cocoa powder
¼ cup (65g) peanut butter
¼ cup (65g) vanilla protein powder
1 tbsp (18ml) rosewater
1 vanilla bean
1 cup (145g) brazil nuts

Steps

1. Using a food processor, blend the cocoa powder, peanut butter, protein powder, rosewater, and vanilla into a thick mixture.
2. Place a heaped spoonful of the mixture on a plate and then roll it to form a 2" (5cm) ball. You may need to add extra spoons to properly form the ball shape.
3. Chop the brazil nuts and spread them out onto a plate.
4. Take each ball and individually roll them on the plate of nuts.
5. Place on a tray lined with baking paper.
6. Refrigerate for an hour.

Shopping list

Purchase specialty ingredients on Amazon:

Unsweetened cocoa powder:	https://amzn.to/2uq0sgr
Peanut butter:	https://amzn.to/2uhz6bZ
Vanilla protein powder:	https://amzn.to/2u7ngC9
Rose water:	https://amzn.to/2znjg5l
Vanilla bean:	https://amzn.to/2KSuOCd
Brazil nuts:	https://amzn.to/2JbZiuk

Nutritional information (per serving)

Calories 102 (From Fat 77)
Total Fat 8.5g (daily 13%)
Saturated Fat 2.0g (daily 10%)
Cholesterol 7mg (daily 02%)
Sodium 29mg (daily 01%)
Potassium 128mg (daily 04%)
Carbohydrates 2.9g (daily 01%)
Dietary Fiber 1.4g (daily 06%)
Sugars 0.8g
Protein 5.5g

11) No Cook Cocoa Bars

These lovely bars are the perfect on-the-go treat. They also don't require any cooking.

Net carbs: 2.2g per bar
Makes 6 bars

Ingredients

4 tbsp (55g) coconut butter
8 tbsp (116g) cream cheese
1 tbsp (7g) unsweetened cocoa powder
6 tbsp (44g) vanilla protein powder
¼ cup (20g) organic chocolate pieces (70% cocoa)*
*You can use other chocolates, but select ones with a high cocoa value, as these have less sugar and so lower carb counts.

Steps

1. Mix the coconut butter and cream cheese.
2. Add the cocoa powder and protein powder.
3. Mix until completely combined. You may need to use your hands.
4. Grate the chocolate pieces over the mixture.
5. Continue mixing to ensure all the ingredients are fully combined.
6. Line a baking tin with baking paper.
7. Pour the mixture into the tin.
8. Refrigerate for approximately 15 minutes. It shouldn't become hard, the goal is simply to chill it.

Shopping list

Purchase specialty ingredients on Amazon:

Coconut butter:	https://amzn.to/2ujMtbT
Cream cheese:	https://amzn.to/2uiTn0L
Unsweetened cocoa powder:	https://amzn.to/2uq0sgr
Vanilla protein powder:	https://amzn.to/2u7ngC9
Organic chocolate pieces (70% cocoa) (not always available)	https://amzn.to/2NCGTKr

Nutritional information (per serving)

Calories 64	(from Fat 50)
Total Fat 5.6g	(daily 9%)
Saturated Fat 3.6g	(daily 18%)
Cholesterol 15mg	(daily 5%)
Sodium 42mg	(daily 2%)
Potassium 31mg	(daily 1%)
Carbohydrates 2.3g	(daily 1%)
Dietary Fiber 0.1g	(daily 0%)
Sugars 1.7g	
Protein 1.3g	

12) Almond Pie Crust

On it's own, this pie crust isn't sweet. However, it is the perfect substitute for other desserts that require a base. Checkout the next cheese cake, cinnamon berry pie, creamy lemon pie and pumpkin pie recipes for inspiration.

Net carbs: 0.5g per serving
Makes 8 servings

Ingredients

3 tbsp (43g) butter
1½ cups (145g) almond flour

Steps

1. Preheat the oven to 350°F (180°C).
2. In a saucepan, melt the butter.
3. Add the almond flour and stir briefly.
4. Pour into a pie tin.
5. Use the back of a spatula to smooth it out.
6. Bake for 10 minutes until the crust starts to brown. After the first 5 minutes, check regularly, as it burns very quickly.

Shopping list

Purchase specialty ingredients on Amazon:

Almond flour: https://amzn.to/2MXcd5t

Nutritional information (per serving)

Calories 68 (from Fat 63)
Total Fat 7.0g (daily 11%)
Saturated Fat 2.9g (daily 15%)
Cholesterol 11mg (daily 4%)
Sodium 33mg (daily 1%)
Potassium 1mg (daily 0%)
Carbohydrates 1.1g (daily 0%)
Dietary Fiber 0.6g (daily 2%)
Sugars 0.2g
Protein 1.2g

13) Cheesecake

A classic favorite. This uses the almond pie crust from the previous recipe.

Net carbs: 8.2g per serving (including pie crust)
Makes 8 servings

Ingredients

8oz (60g) low fat cream cheese
1 vanilla bean
¼ cup (40g) raisins
2 cups (470g) heavy cream (double cream)
1 almond pie crust (see previous recipe)

Steps

7. In a bowl, beat the cream cheese and vanilla for approximately 2 minutes until smooth.
1. Using a food processor, blend the raisins.
2. In a separate bowl add the blended raisins and heavy cream. Whisk at a high speed to form a stiff mixture.
3. Combine the two mixtures. Gently fold by hand.
4. Pour the mixture into the almond pie crust.
5. Refrigerate until set.

Shopping list

Purchase specialty ingredients on Amazon:

Low fat cream cheese: https://amzn.to/2L2fAre

Vanilla bean: https://amzn.to/2KSuOCd

Raisins: https://amzn.to/2zy4tFp

Nutritional information (per serving)

Calories 489 (from Fat 420)
Total Fat 46.7g (daily 72%)
Saturated Fat 20.6g 1 (daily 3%)
Cholesterol 99mg (daily 33%)
Sodium 209mg (daily 9%)
Potassium 254mg (daily 7%)
Carbohydrates 11.6g (daily 4%)
Dietary Fiber 3.4g (daily 14%)
Sugars 4.7g • Protein 9.4g
(Includes values from almond pie crust)

14) Cinnamon Berry Pie

A berry party for your tongue! This uses the almond pie crust (see earlier recipe).

Net carbs: 6.3g per serving (including pie crust)
Makes 8 servings

Ingredients

4 cups (400g) mixed berries (strawberries, raspberries, blueberries)
¼ tsp (1.5g) sea salt
¾ cup (175ml) water
4 tsp (30g) arrowroot starch (or corn starch)
1 tbsp (13g) coconut oil
1 tbsp (7.8g) cinnamon powder
1 almond pie crust (see earlier recipe)

Steps

1. Add one quarter of the berries, sea salt and water to a medium sized saucepan.
2. Bring the saucepan to a boil and then cook while stirring.
3. After 3 minutes, the berries should soften, so add the arrowroot starch and stir until fully dissolved.
4. Add the coconut oil and continue stirring.
5. When the coconut oil has completely dissolved add the remaining berries.
6. Continue stirring until the berries soften.
7. Add the cinnamon powder.
8. Pour the mixture into the almond pie crust.
9. Refrigerate until set.

Shopping list

Purchase specialty ingredients on Amazon:

Mixed berries:	**https://amzn.to/2NCXeyB**
Arrowroot starch: (not always available)	**https://amzn.to/2znB0xt**
Corn starch:	**https://amzn.to/2NDXSw6**
Coconut oil:	**https://amzn.to/2NwYOCl**
Cinnamon powder:	**https://amzn.to/2J5Bqs8**

Nutritional information (per serving)

Calories 122	(from Fat 85)
Total Fat 9.4g	(daily 14%)
Saturated Fat 5.5g	(daily 28%)
Cholesterol 4mg	(daily 01%)
Sodium 304mg	(daily 13%)
Potassium 69mg	(daily 02%)
Carbohydrates 9.1g	(daily 03%)
Dietary Fiber 2.8g	(daily 11%)
Sugars 3.8g	
Protein 1.5g	

(Includes values from almond pie crust)

15) Creamy Lemon Pie

Yummy.... This classic lemon pie is irresistible. This uses the almond pie crust (see earlier recipe).

Net carbs: 11.1g per serving (including pie crust)
Makes 8 servings

Ingredients

5 large (285g) eggs
¼ cup (85g) honey
⅔ cup (150ml) heavy cream (double cream) for main cream
3 medium (174g) lemons
1 almond pie crust (see earlier recipe)
¼ cup (50ml) additional heavy cream (double cream) for topping

Steps

1. Preheat the oven to 320°F (160°C).
2. Lightly whisk the eggs and honey.
3. Add the cream and gently whisk.
4. Using a grater, remove the zest from the lemons.
5. Squeeze the juice from the lemons.
6. Add the lemon juice and zest to the mixing bowl.
7. Mix until completely combined.
8. Pour the mixture into the almond pie crust.
9. Bake for approximately 40 minutes. When ready, the mixture shouldn't be too liquid.
10. Allow to cool.
11. Whip the additional heavy cream and use it to cover the pie.
12. Place pieces of lemon on top for an extra zingy taste.

Nutritional information (per serving)

Calories 231 (from Fat 172)
Total Fat 19.1g (daily 29%)
Saturated Fat 9.6g (daily 48%)
Cholesterol 148mg (daily 49%)
Sodium 81mg (daily 03%)
Potassium 77mg (daily 02%)
Carbohydrates 12.0g (daily 04%)
Dietary Fiber 0.9g (daily 04%)
Sugars 9.7g
Protein 5.3g
(Includes values from almond pie crust)

16) Pumpkin Pie

Bring the richness of autumn with this lovely Pumpkin Pie! This uses the almond pie crust (see earlier recipe).

Net carbs: 13.4g per serving (including pie crust)
Makes 8 servings

Ingredients

2 large (114g) eggs
1 cup (250g) pumpkin pieces
¾ cup (90g) heavy cream
5 tbsp (106g) honey
1 vanilla bean
½ tsp (3g) salt
1 tsp (2.6g) cinnamon
½ tsp (1.3g) nutmeg
½ tsp (1.3g) allspice
1 almond pie crust (see earlier recipe)

Steps

1. Preheat oven to 350°F (180°C).
2. Slightly beat the eggs
3. Using a food processor, blend the pumpkin pieces.
4. Pour the blended pieces into a bowl.
5. Add the heavy cream and eggs and mix.
6. Add the honey, vanilla, salt, cinnamon, nutmeg and allspice. Mix until completely combined.
7. Pour the mixture into the almond pie crust.
8. Refrigerate until set.

Shopping list

Purchase specialty ingredients on Amazon:

Vanilla bean:	https://amzn.to/2KSuOCd
Cinnamon:	https://amzn.to/2MYXx60
Nutmeg:	https://amzn.to/2L1x61U
Allspice:	https://amzn.to/2J7i31M

Nutritional information (per serving)

Calories 166 (from Fat 104)
Total Fat 11.5g (daily 18%)
Saturated Fat 5.9g (daily 29%)
Cholesterol 68mg (daily 23%)
Sodium 201mg (daily 8%)
Potassium 98mg (daily 3%)
Carbohydrates 14.9g (daily 5%)
Dietary Fiber 1.5g (daily 6%)
Sugars 12.1g
Protein 2.8g
(Includes values from almond pie crust)

17) Crumbling Nutmeg Muffins

These muffins have such a wonderful texture that they bring enjoyment from the moment you touch them.

Net carbs: 4.1g per muffin
Makes 8 muffins

Ingredients

Muffin
6 large (342g) eggs
1 cup (225ml) almond milk
2 tbsp (36ml) lemon juice
1 tbsp (6g) lemon zest
½ cup (50g) coconut oil
⅔ cup (75g) coconut flour

Topping
2 tbsp raw (25g) coconut crystals
2 tbsp (14g) coconut flour
1 tsp (2.6g) nutmeg

Steps

1. Preheat the oven to 350°F (180°C).
2. Lightly grease a muffin tray.
3. Using a food processor, blend the eggs.
4. Add the almond milk, lemon juice and lemon zest. Blend for approximately 1 minute to ensure all is mixed.
5. Gently warm the coconut oil so it fully melts. Avoid too much heat to prevent burning.
6. Add the coconut oil. Again, blend for another minute.
7. Add the coconut flour and gently blend again to ensure it is fully mixed.
8. Pour the mixture into the muffin tray.
9. Bake for approximately 40 minutes.
10. Allow to cool.
11. In a bowl, fully mix the coconut crystals, coconut flour and nutmeg.

12. Spread the topping on the muffins. Use the back of a spatula to ensure smoothness.

Shopping list

Purchase specialty ingredients on Amazon:

Almond milk:	https://amzn.to/2znvVW5
Coconut oil:	https://amzn.to/2NwYOCl
Coconut flour:	https://amzn.to/2KZ9QSj
Coconut crystals:	https://amzn.to/2NAL2i9
Nutmeg:	https://amzn.to/2L1x61U

Nutritional information (per serving)

Calories 235	(From Fat 183)
Total Fat 20.3g	(daily 31%)
Saturated Fat 15.1g	(daily 75%)
Cholesterol 130mg	(daily 43%)
Sodium 72mg	(daily 3%)
Potassium 128mg	(daily 4%)
Carbohydrates 8.9g	(daily 3%)
Dietary Fiber 4.8g	(daily 19%)
Sugars 1.4g	
Protein 6.2g	

18) Cinnamon Muffins

Lovely cinnamon muffins that are easy to make.

Net carbs: 1.2g carbs per muffin
Makes 12 muffins

Ingredients

2 tsp (9.6g) baking powder
1 tbsp (7.8g) cinnamon
2 cups (240g) coconut flour
¼ tsp (1.5g) sea salt
2 tbsp (14g) coconut oil
2 tbsp (36ml) coconut milk
4 large (228g) eggs
⅓ cup (75ml) water

Steps

1. Preheat the oven to 350°F (180°C).
2. Mix the baking powder, cinnamon, coconut flour and sea salt until completely combined.
3. Gently warm the coconut oil so it fully melts. Avoid too much heat to prevent burning.
4. In a separate bowl, mix the warmed coconut oil, coconut milk, eggs and water. Again, these should fully combine.
5. Combine the two mixtures.
6. Have a final round of mixing to again ensure all ingredients have combined.
7. Lightly butter a muffin tin.
8. Pour the mixture into the tin.
9. Bake for approximately 15 to 20 minutes.

Shopping list

Purchase specialty ingredients on Amazon:

Cinnamon powder:	https://amzn.to/2J5Bqs8
Coconut flour:	https://amzn.to/2KZ9QSj
Coconut oil:	https://amzn.to/2NwYOCl
Coconut milk:	https://amzn.to/2KVFPmw

Nutritional information (per serving)

Calories 81	(From Fat 64)
Total Fat 7.1g	(daily 11%)
Saturated Fat 3.1g	(daily 16%)
Cholesterol 55mg	(daily 18%)
Sodium 218mg	(daily 9%)
Potassium 113mg	(daily 3%)
Carbohydrates 2.3g	(daily 1%)
Dietary Fiber 1.0g	(daily 4%)
Sugars 0.4g	
Protein 3.1g	

19) Mixed Berry Layer Cake

A unique combination of two recipes to make an irresistible third.

Net carbs: 4.8g per serving (includes Cinnamon Muffin and Mixed Berry Fool Values)
Makes 8 servings

Ingredients

This recipe is a combination of the previous Mixed Berry Fool and Cinnamon Muffin recipes. There are a couple of changes as detailed below.

Steps

1. Make the Mixed Berry Fool but keep the mixture in a bowl.
2. Follow the steps of the Cinnamon Muffin recipe, but omit the cinnamon. Bake the mixture in one large cake tin as opposed to individual muffin tins.
3. When the cake is ready, allow it to cool.
4. Split the cake into two layers.
5. Pour three quarters of the Mixed Berry Fool on top of the first cake layer.
6. Place the second layer on top.
7. Spread the remaining Mixed Berry Fool on top of the completed cake.

Nutritional information (per serving)

Calories 185 (From Fat 148)
Total Fat 16.4g (daily 25%)
Saturated Fat 8.2g (daily 41%)
Cholesterol 102mg (daily 34%)
Sodium 333mg (daily 14%)
Potassium 249mg (daily 07%)
Carbohydrates 6.8g (daily 02%)
Dietary Fiber 2.0g (daily 08%)
Sugars 2.9g
Protein 5.3g
(includes Cinnamon Muffin and Mixed Berry Fool Values)

20) Berry Chocolate Cake

This cake is made in 3 parts. The effort is worth it because it is absolutely delicious!

Net carbs: 12g per serving
Makes 12 servings

Ingredients

For the cake:
½ cup (120g) almond flour
2 tsp (9.6g) baking powder
2 tbsp (15g) unsweetened cocoa powder
1 cup (100g) chopped nuts
2 tbsp (30ml) honey
¼ tsp (1.5g) salt
1 vanilla bean
6 medium (318g) eggs

For the icing:
3oz (80g) unsalted butter
7oz (200g) cream cheese
1.5oz (40ml) heavy cream (double cream)
1 vanilla bean
2 tbsp (30g) unsweetened cocoa powder
3 tbsp (44ml) honey
1 tsp (2.6g) cinnamon

For the berry topping:
3 cups (375g) mixed berries (strawberries, raspberries, blueberries)

Steps

To make the cake:
1. Preheat the oven to 375°F (190°C).
2. Mix the almond flour, baking powder, cocoa powder, chopped nuts, honey, salt and vanilla.
3. In a separate bowl, gently mix the eggs, then add them to the main bowl.
4. Grease a cake tin.
5. Pour the mixture into the tin.
6. Cook for approximately 20 minutes. The cake should be springy but firm.

To make the icing:
1. Mix the butter, the cream cheese, heavy cream and vanilla. For best results, before mixing, leave the butter out for a few hours so it becomes soft.
2. Once mixed, add the cocoa powder, honey and cinnamon.
3. Mix until all ingredients have completely combined. However, take care to ensure it does not become too liquid.

To make the berry topping:
1. Take half the berries and use a food processor to blend them into a thick sauce.
2. Only half the berries should be blended. The remaining berries will be used for decoration.

To assemble the finished cake:
1. Allow the cake to fully cool.
2. Pour the icing over the cake covering it fully.
3. Use the back of a spatula to pat the mixture down.
4. Take a spoon of the blended berry mixture and pour it on top of the cake. Use the back of a spatula to spread it over. Gradually add the blended mixture one spoon at a time. Take care not to put too much on at once to stop the cake from becoming too wet.
5. Only half the berries were blended to make the sauce. Take the remaining berries and place them on top of the cake to decorate it.

Shopping list

Purchase specialty ingredients on Amazon:

Almond flour:	https://amzn.to/2MXcd5t
Unsweetened cocoa powder:	https://amzn.to/2uq0sgr
Vanilla bean:	https://amzn.to/2ueRMcD
Cream cheese:	https://amzn.to/2uiTn0L
Mixed berries:	https://amzn.to/2NCXeyB

Nutritional information (per serving)

Calories 267 (From Fat 193)
Total Fat 21.4g (daily 33%)
Saturated Fat 9.1g (daily 46%)
Cholesterol 119mg (daily 40%)
Sodium 173mg (daily 7%)
Potassium 253mg (daily 7%)
Carbohydrates 14.6g (daily 5%)
Dietary Fiber 2.6g (daily 10%)
Sugars 9.9g
Protein 7.4g

21) Apricot Cocoa Cake

Lovely chocolate-like taste with an apricot twist.

Net carbs: 9.3g per serving
Makes 12 servings

Ingredients

10 apricots
1 medium (120g) banana
½ cup (110ml) coconut oil
1 cup (250g) unsweetened cocoa powder
2 large (114g) eggs
1 vanilla bean
½ cup (55g) almond flour
1 tsp (4.8g) baking soda
½ tsp (3g) sea salt

Steps

1. Preheat the oven to 350°F (180°C).
2. Using a food processor, blend the apricots into a purée.
3. Add the banana. Continue blending until puréed.
4. Pour the purée into a mixing bowl.
5. Gently warm the coconut oil so it fully melts. Avoid too much heat to prevent burning.
6. Add the melted coconut oil, cocoa powder, eggs and vanilla. Mix until all has combined.
7. In a separate bowl, add the almond flour, baking soda, sea salt and remaining cocoa powder. Again, mix until all have combined.
8. Merge the two bowls and gently mix until smooth.
9. Greece a baking tray and pour in the mixture. Use the back of a spatula to smooth down the top.
10. Bake for approximately 30 minutes. When ready, you can put a knife in it and it will come out clean.

Shopping list

Purchase specialty ingredients on Amazon:

Apricots:	https://amzn.to/2NBNBQI
Coconut oil:	https://amzn.to/2NwYOCI
Almond flour:	
Vanilla bean:	https://amzn.to/2KSuOCd
Unsweetened cocoa powder:	https://amzn.to/2uq0sgr

Nutritional information

Calories 161	(from Fat 116)
Total Fat 12.9g	(daily 20%)
Saturated Fat 9.3g	(daily 46%)
Cholesterol 27mg	(daily 09%)
Sodium 120mg	(daily 05%)
Potassium 438mg	(daily 13%)
Carbohydrates 17.2g	(daily 06%)
Dietary Fiber 7.9g	(daily 32%)
Sugars 4.3g	
Protein 5.8g	

22) Carrot Cake

A well loved classic.

Net carbs: 5g per serving
Makes 16 servings

Ingredients

1 cup (209g) coconut oil
5 large (285g) eggs
3 tbsp (44ml) honey
1 vanilla bean
½ cup (45g) brazil nuts
3 cups (150g) grated carrot
½ cup (65g) walnuts
1½ cup (145g) almond flour
2 tsp (9.6g) baking powder
2 tsp (5.2g) cinnamon

Steps

1. Preheat the oven to 340°F (170°C).
2. Gently warm the coconut oil so it fully melts. Avoid too much heat to prevent burning.
3. Whisk the eggs, honey and vanilla.
4. Add the brazil nuts, carrot and walnuts and mix well.
5. Add the almond flour, baking powder and cinnamon. Mix until completely combined.
6. Pour the mixture into a loaf tin.
7. Bake for approximately 40 minutes. When ready, you can put a knife in the centre and it will come out clean.

Shopping list

Purchase specialty ingredients on Amazon:

Coconut oil:	https://amzn.to/2NwYOCl
Vanilla bean:	https://amzn.to/2KSuOCd
Brazil nuts:	https://amzn.to/2JbZiuk
Walnuts:	https://amzn.to/2u5RJk5
Almond flour:	https://amzn.to/2MXcd5t
Cinnamon powder:	https://amzn.to/2J5Bqs8

Nutritional information (per serving)

Calories 213 (from Fat 185)
Total Fat 20.6g (daily 32%)
Saturated Fat 12.9g (daily 64%)
Cholesterol 51mg (daily 17%)
Sodium 31mg (daily 01%)
Potassium 136mg (daily 04%)
Carbohydrates 6.1g (daily 02%)
Dietary Fiber 1.1g (daily 04%)
Sugars 4.0g
Protein 3.8g

Easily rewire your mindset: Use desserts as tools to both succeed at your diet and change your whole life

- Do you have unhealthy eating habits?
- Do you binge on junk food?
- Do you tend to over-eat and over-indulge?
- Do you try very hard to eat healthily, but find it hard to maintain self-control?

While the desserts in this book are both delicious and low in carbs, you can still put on weight by overindulging in them.

Bad eating habits are often caused by a lack of satisfaction in life. Your mind and body crave unhealthy food for instant satisfaction. Unfortunately, this creates a vicious circle. The unhealthy food makes you overweight, which further reduces satisfaction while increasing the likelihood of over-indulging.

Thankfully, by making a few simple changes, you can rewire your mindset and use desserts as tools to not only help you to succeed at weight loss but also to form good habits for a better life overall.

In the following pages, we examine 5 mindset tools:
- Make desserts a reward for forming new habits
- Dessert scheduling
- Savor preparation
- Make dessert eating a ritual
- Form the habit of gratitude

Mindset tool 1:
Make desserts a reward for forming new habits

The act of forming a single new habit, even one that is not connected to weight loss, gives invaluable skills that make dieting much easier.

Desserts can act as a powerful motivational reward. Here is a 6-step plan for using desserts to form new habits:

1. Select a habit

Pick a habit you want to achieve. Make sure it has a specific measurement.

For example:
- Exercising for 10 minutes every day
- Drinking 8 glasses of water each day
- Spending 20 minutes a day reading a self-help book

To increase your chance of success, only tackle one habit at a time.

2. Set a visual target

Get a calendar and put it where you will see it each day. It can be a paper calendar for your wall or a calendar app on your phone. Whatever you use, you must be able to see it each day without making the effort to open it.

3. Select a timeframe

Pick a deadline for your habit. Select a dessert from this book to use as a reward. Write the dessert name on the deadline date.

It generally takes 21 days to form a new habit. However, for your first attempt, it might be better to set a smaller deadline, such as seven or even three days.

Be sure to put your goal on a calendar, as if you keep it in your head, it will weigh your mind down making it harder to achieve.

4. Maintain your progress

Mark off each day as you progress to your goal.

If you skip a day, keep going. A habit is only broken if you skip it two days in a row. Instead of beating yourself up for missing a day, use that emotion to fuel your determination so you don't skip tomorrow!

5. Succeed!

When you reach your goal, enjoy your dessert!
If you fail to reach your goal, then write down the factors that stopped you. By writing down these factors and thinking about them, your mind will come up with solutions. Turn these insights into an action plan to succeed on a second attempt.

If you fail your goal, then you cannot have the dessert. However, you can allow yourself to have a smaller treat provided you have a written plan to help you succeed next time. Again, writing down the steps (either on paper on a computer) is important, as if you keep them in your head, they won't be effective.

6. Extend the process

Once you've formed a few habits, use the process to realize your dreams, by breaking them down into smaller habits.

For example, you might have the dream of starting your own fashion business. You could break this down into goals such as:
- "Spending 10 minutes each day posting in a Facebook business group"
  – as this will help you gather tips on starting a business.
- "Spending 10 minutes sharing fashion tips in a Facebook fashion group"
  – as this will help you build a following. It will also help you understand customer desires.

You can achieve any dream by breaking it down into smaller steps. Don't worry about not knowing all the steps – just start and the answers will come.

Mindset tool 2:
Dessert scheduling

It's a lot easier to avoid random binges on junk food if you know that you have a planned time for eating desserts that is only a few days away. Therefore, in addition to using desserts as rewards for achieving new habits, you should also have scheduled days each week for eating desserts.

There are 20 recipes in this book, so a good tip is to make a list of your 10 "must-have" desserts and save these as rewards for good habits. Then schedule the remaining 10 as regular treats. That way, you have the incentive to work for your must-haves, but can still enjoy treats on a regular basis.

Mindset tool 3:
Savor preparation

Savor the process of preparing a dessert. Begin this from the moment you unwrap the raw ingredients and continue all the way to baking the dishes and allowing them to cool.

- How do the ingredients feel in your hands?
- What patterns can you see in the textures of the ingredients?
- Do these patterns remind you of anything interesting?
- What differences in colors can you identify between each ingredient?
- How do the patterns and colors change as the ingredients are cooked?
- What aromas do they make when you bake them?
- How do the aromas feel as they enter your lungs?
- What emotions do they create?
- What memories do they trigger?

This form of reflection might seem like hippy-nonsense. However, savoring the preparation process creates a unique form of happiness. It provides satisfaction, lowering the impulse to binge and eat unhealthy.

Mindset tool 4:
Make dessert eating a ritual

Our society has little respect for food. We often combine eating with other activities such as driving, watching TV, surfing the Internet or doing other work.

It is important to make eating a ritual. This can either be privately or with friends.

Binge eating occurs because it provides instant satisfaction. If you make dessert eating a ritual, then binge eating loses appeal, as it lacks the deeper emotional experience that a ritual creates.

Private rituals

Busy modern lifestyles make 'me-time' vital. When eating a dessert, consider making it a private ritual.

Before eating, look for ways to relax yourself. For example:
- Doing deep breathing
- Taking a warm bath
- Reading your favorite book
- Listening to your favorite song

Ensure your environment allows you to savor the dessert. For example:
- Sit in a comfortable chair
- Look out of the window (if you have something interesting to look at)
- Sit in a quiet room

When eating, slowly savor the dessert. Pay attention to the taste of every bite. Doing this will fill you with satisfaction, lowering the motive to eat unhealthy.

Social rituals

Sharing desserts with friends is also important. Research by Dr Barbara Fredrickson from the University of North Carolina shows that being with friends activates the immune system and encourages good health. Desserts are a powerful way to enhance the social experience.

In addition, if you take care to make only one dessert, then there will be no pieces left over, so you don't have to worry about binge eating!

You can get friends and family involved with the preparation process to further enhance the experience.

However, a study by N.A. Christakis and J.H. Fowler in the New England Journal of Medicine (2007) shows that overweight people tend to socialize together. As the famous entrepreneur Jim Rohn states, you are the average of the 5 people you spend the most time with, so if you have lots of obese friends, then eating food with them could encourage over-eating.

Mindset tool 5:
Form the habit of gratitude

"I'll be grateful when I am happy." – This is a common belief held by most people.

In reality, gratitude creates happiness. As the neuropsychologist Donald Hebb states, "neurons that fire together, wire together". This might sound like hippy nonsense, but there's a rational explanation for it:

How your brain works

Your brain faces two key challenges.

Firstly, it can only pay attention to a small number of thoughts.

Secondly, the world is filled with an abundance of details and there are too many for your brain to pay attention to all of them.

Take something simple such as a shirt: It has multiple details, including stitching, buttons, labels, cuffs, buttonholes, a collar, creases, and patterns. Each one of these elements also have multiple details. A single button, for example, has tiny scratches, threads to hold it down and different textures. Your brain cannot pay attention to all these details.

Your brain copes in two ways. It first prioritizes the thoughts in your head. Once it has done that, it then filters out most of the details in the world, only paying attention to those that mirror your thoughts.

If you've ever missed something that was right in front of you, it's usually because you've been preoccupied with other thoughts, so your brain filtered out the new object.

The power of gratitude

By being grateful, you can prioritize gratitude in your mind.
Your brain will then direct attention to opportunities for happiness in your environment.

If your mind is filled with worries, stress, deadlines or negative impulses, then your brain will filter out opportunities for happiness.

A good way to form gratitude is through daily journaling. At the end of each day, recall 5 events you were grateful for and write them down. They have to be written down as if you keep them in your mind, they will get lost amongst other thoughts. However, typing them on a computer, tablet or mobile works just as well as using paper.

Forming this habit results in increased happiness and life satisfaction, which lowers the impulse to eat unhealthily.

Free Gift + Free Future Books: Expires soon!

Congratulations! If you can read this message, then your purchase qualifies for the free *Suggested Accompaniments* chart.

Have you ever wanted to add something to your dessert? Maybe:
- A few blueberries on the side?
- A scoop of ice cream?
- A sprinkling of nuts?
- A spray of cream?

Be careful! These additions could massively inflate your carb and calorie intake!

Our chart illustrates the carb and calorie values of the most popular dessert accompaniments. It is elegantly designed, so you can print it out and pin it up in your kitchen for easy access to this vital information. That way, you'll know exactly which additions are safe to have!

This free gift will be deleted from future editions of the book and sold as a separate item with an RRP of $9.99. When this happens, it will no longer be free for you, so please take action now to secure your copy.

To receive your gift, simply validate your email address at
http://bit.ly/lowcarbclub

In order to receive your gift, you will need to sign up for our free email newsletter, which details our new books. Don't worry about spam: We only send the newsletter occasionally, usually once a year.

Don't undo all your hard work with an innocent mistake. Download today!

Join my Facebook recipe group!

My Facebook group is a great place to:
- Hang out with other cookbook readers
- Get reading suggestions for other authors
- Get special offers on my books.

My group will be launching later in the year, but you can use this exclusive link to join now and be a **VIP member**:

Join now:
http://bit.ly/recipe-group

(My group is completely free.)

Check out my other dessert books

Baking Magic:
The best cakes, cookies, and desserts recipes

• The very best recipes
• Step-by-step instructions
• Mouthwatering dishes, such as Chocolate Mousse Crêpes Cake, Pink Swirls Ombré Cake, Peppermint Truffles, and Giant Pizza Cookies!

Weave baking magic!

Learn more:
http://bit.ly/bakingmagicbook

Hawaiian Baking:
Baking Magic 2

• The very best Hawaiian desserts recipes
• Step-by-step instructions
• Mouthwatering dishes, such as Chantilly Chocolate Chiffon Cake, Mango and Macadamia Hawaiian Cookies, Haupia and Chocolate Pie, Green Tea Fairy Cakes, and Chantilly Red Bean Paste Pancakes!

Learn more:
bit.ly/bakingmagicbook2

Baking with Ice Cream: Baking Magic 3

- The very best recipes that use ice cream!
- Step by step instructions
- Enchanting dishes, including Pumpkin Ice Cream Pie, Nougat Meringue Ice Cream Cake, Neapolitan Banana Split Ice Cream Cake, Toasted Marshmallow Ice Cream Cake, Salty Peanut & Pretzel Ice Cream Cake and Chocolate & Coconut Sorbet Baked Alaska!

Learn more:
http://bit.ly/bakingmagicbook3

Check out my dessert mystery books

A collection of cozy cat mysteries that feature all the desserts from my recipe books.

Fairy Cake Fatality
**Fairy cakes, a kitten, magic, and a murder in England
...all with a fairy twist!**

(The Cake Fairy Mysteries – Book 1)

Faye left California to start a new life in England. Things aren't going well and her new cake shop is close to bankruptcy, but she gets a lucky break when she is chosen to be featured on the town's popular radio program. Unfortunately, on the day of the recording, a murder occurs and she is the prime suspect!

She tries to solve the case herself, but each clue she finds leaves her more confused. To make things worse, she keeps having hallucinations about being a fairy, but these only occur when a certain kitten is around. Or maybe there is something to these visions? Can Faye befriend the kitten and master her fairy past while solving the case?

Learn more:
http://bit.ly/fairycake1

Fairy Cake Betrayal
Fairy cakes, a kitten, magic, and an impossible murder in Hawaii …all with a fairy twist!

(The Cake Fairy Mysteries – Book 2)

Faye Anderson is searching for her mother, who mysteriously disappeared over a decade ago. The quest takes Faye to Hawaii, where she stumbles upon a shadowy killer fleeing a murder scene. Unfortunately, the killer seems to be none other than her own mother. Worse still, when the police arrive, there don't seem to be any signs that a murder has taken place. There are no witnesses, and even the body is missing!

It's an impossible case, but Faye isn't going to let that stop her, especially when she can draw on her fairy powers, as well as the help of Tom, her newly adopted pet cat. But the island of Hawaii holds many unwanted secrets, such as the story behind her mom's disappearance and the truth about Tom's past. Solving the crime could lead to the ultimate betrayal…

Learn more:
http://bit.ly/fairycake2

Fairy Cake Faker
Fairy cakes, a kitten, magic, and a murder to prevent in England ...all with a fairy twist!

(The Cake Fairy Mysteries – Book 3)

Things should finally be going well for Faye Anderson. After all, her struggling cake shop is starting to make a profit. Her life, at last, seems to be in balance.

Except her pet cat Tom keeps on having nightmares that suggest something terrible is about to occur.

And when Faye finds the body of a dear friend, she realizes that more murders are about to hit the sleepy town of Fairfields.

It's going to be a tricky case to solve, especially since there doesn't seem to be any clues. Can Faye find the culprit before disaster strikes?

Learn more:
http://bit.ly/fairycake3

Enjoy this book: Yes/No?
– Contact the author

If you enjoyed the book...

If you enjoyed this book, please leave a review on Amazon.

I am just a regular girl and so don't have the time or money to compete with established publishers. Posting a review would help me greatly!!

Please leave your review here:
http://bit.ly/lowcarbreview

(You will be asked to sign in to your Amazon account.)

If you disliked the book...

I really want you to enjoy this book. So if you have any issues, please contact me (the author) directly, and I will fix your issue!

Email: sabrina.hartford.books@gmail.com

I will personally respond to your email as soon as possible. Your feedback will also be considered for future updates. These updates will be provided FREE of charge to all existing readers.

The Cake Fairy Store

**A range of limited edition products based on The Cake Fairy series. This range is always being updated.
Visit http://bit.ly/cake-fairy-store for the latest.**

Tom and cakes 1

Limited edition:
Available in a range of colors and sizes.

http://bit.ly/tom-cakes-1

Tom pokes in

Limited edition:
Available in a range of colors and sizes.

http://bit.ly/kitty-poke-shirt

**Over 10 other designs available!
Visit http://bit.ly/cake-fairy-store for the latest.**

Images subject to change. Please visit the links to view the actual product before purchase. Please contact me if you are unable to make a purchase (sabrina.hartford.books@gmail.com).

Freebies & Offers

Honey Bar
Free online discounts + Free Amazon vouchers!

When shopping online, the Honey bar automatically applies discounts to your purchases.

You also receive bonus points, which you can exchange for Amazon gift vouchers!

- Works on many online stores.
- Works in multiple countries, including the US and UK.
- COMPLETELY FREE – No credit card or subscription required.

Install for free when you use this special link:
http://joinhoney.com/ref/ut22e0

Read Kindle books for free

Kindle Unlimited lets you read the vast majority of Kindle books for a low monthly fee. You can try the service FREE for 30 days and cancel the trial without paying a penny.

Use this exclusive link:
http://bit.ly/free-ku

Two free audiobooks

Get two free audiobooks when you sign up for a free 30 day trial of Audible from Amazon.

- Choose 2 free books from over 2 million titles.
- Cancel 30-day free trial without paying a penny.

Use this exclusive link:
http://bit.ly/2-free-audio

About the author

Sabrina Hartford just loves cooking and has been making sweet treats since she was two years old. Seriously, her baby photos show her helping her mama in the kitchen!

She has had a variety of jobs in her time, but now, when she's not following her first love of writing, she enjoys baking, traveling, volunteering, and reading books.

Email: sabrina.hartford.books@gmail.com

Don't forget to leave a review!

If you enjoyed this book, please leave a review on Amazon. I am just a regular girl and so don't have the time or money to compete with established publishers. Posting a review would help me greatly!!

Please leave your review here:
http://bit.ly/lowcarbreview

(You will be asked to sign in to your Amazon account.)

If you didn't like the book, please email me with your comments, as I'd be more than happy to fix or consider any issues you may have.

Email: sabrina.hartford.books@gmail.com

Copyright

Special thanks to Madhu Sharma Ltd in the help given to bring this book to market.

© 2015 Madhu Sharma Ltd

Low Carb Desserts:
Low Carb Dessert Cook Book for Low Carb Diets

Copyright: Madhu Sharma Ltd
Published: 4 September 2015
Publisher: Madhu Sharma Ltd

The right of Madhu Sharma Ltd to be identified as author of this Work has been asserted by Madhu Sharma Ltd in accordance with sections 77 and 78 of the Copyright, Designs and Patents Act 1988.

All rights reserved. No part of this publication may be reproduced, stored in retrieval system, copied in any form or by any means, electronic, mechanical, photocopying, recording or otherwise transmitted without written permission from the publisher. You must not circulate this book in any format.

This book is licensed for your personal enjoyment only. This ebook may not be resold or given away to other people. If you would like to share this book with another person, please purchase an additional copy for each recipient. If you're reading this book and did not purchase it, or it was not purchased for your use only, then please return to amazon.com and purchase your own copy. Thank you for respecting the hard work of this author.

LCD-SE-17jul18

Printed in Great Britain
by Amazon